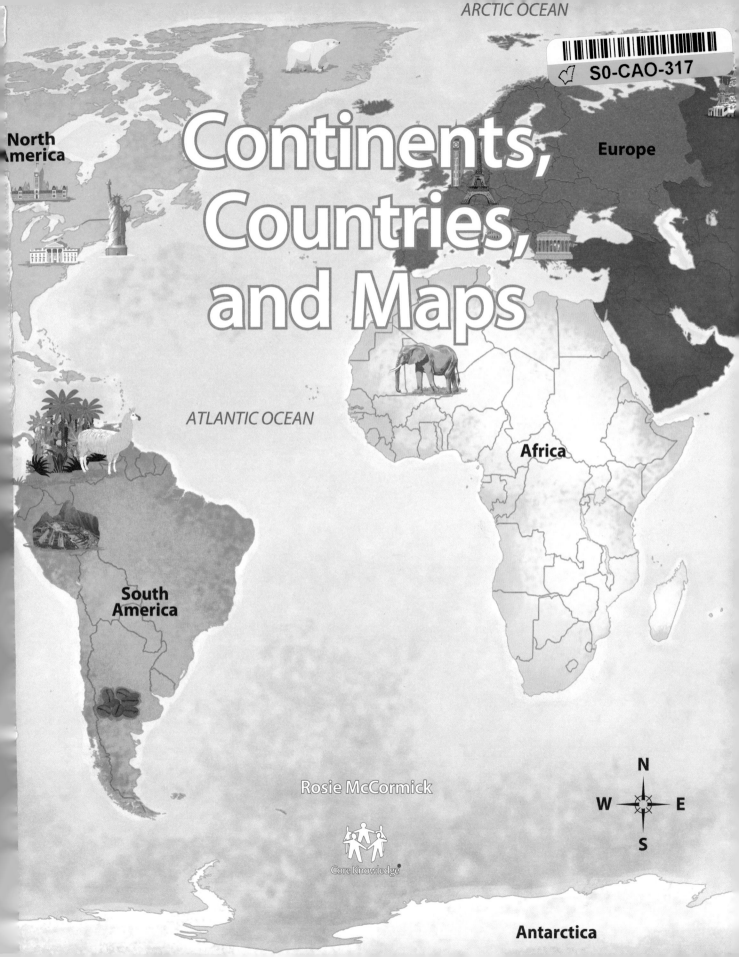

ARCTIC OCEAN

North America

Europe

Continents, Countries, and Maps

ATLANTIC OCEAN

Africa

South America

Rosie McCormick

CoreKnowledge

Antarctica

ISBN: 978-1-68380-382-9

Continents, Countries, and Maps

Table of Contents

Finding Your Way Around

One way to learn about a state, a country, or even the world is to look at maps.

Maps show towns, cities, and places of interest.

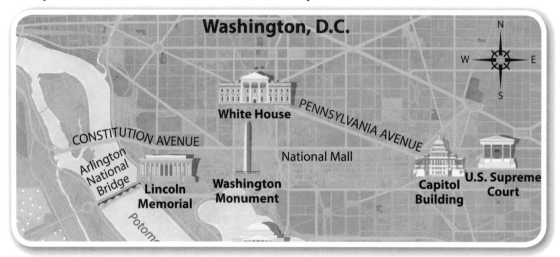

Maps show lakes and rivers.

And maps can even show information about the weather.

Maps show how to get from one place to another. Maps can be made of paper.

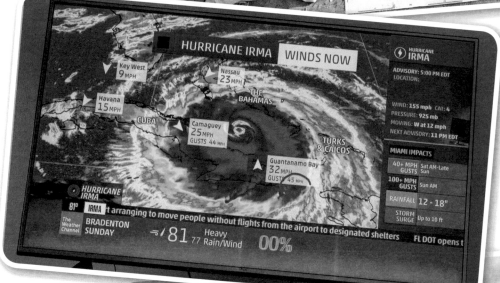

Maps can be shown on TV.

Maps can be viewed on a GPS in a car.

Symbols are used to show important information on a map. The symbols make it easier for us to understand the information. There are symbols for towns, capital cities, mountains, rivers, highways, railroads, and much more. What the symbols mean is explained in a key that is often part of the map.

MAP KEY

Symbol	Meaning	Symbol	Meaning
══	Highway	🌲	Forest
●	Town	▨▨▨	Railroad
⭐	Capital City	▲▲	Mountain
✈	Airport	〰	River
🔥	Campground		

How do we know which way to go? Well, we follow the four main directions, that's how! The four main directions are north, south, east, and west. Maps usually have a compass rose to point out these directions.

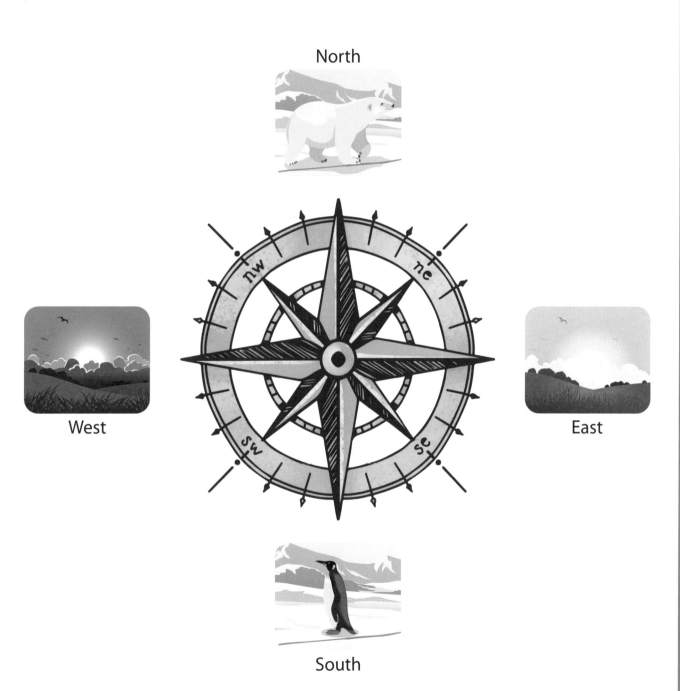

North

West

East

South

There are about two hundred countries in the world. Some countries are islands, but most are found on large areas of land we call continents. There are seven continents on Earth. You can see the seven continents on this map of the world.

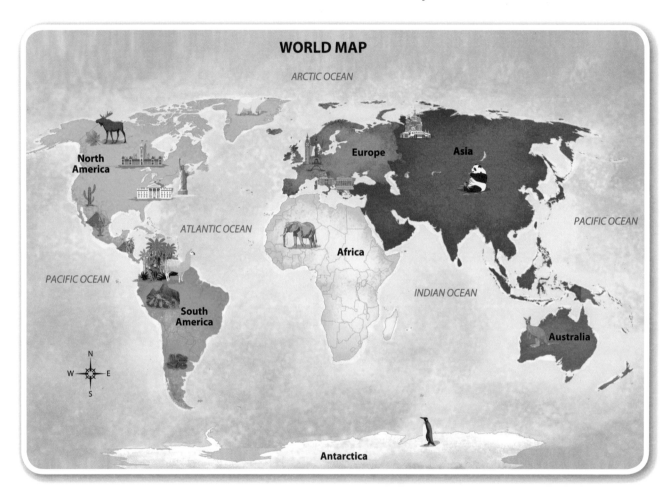

Much of Earth is covered by oceans and seas. The oceans are the Pacific, the Atlantic, the Indian, and the Arctic.

We sometimes show Earth as a round globe because Earth is a round planet! The center or middle of Earth's surface is marked by a line called the equator. Earth's northern half is called the Northern Hemisphere, and the southern half is called the Southern Hemisphere. The farthest northern point is the North Pole. The farthest southern point is the South Pole.

North America: The United States

The United States is part of North America, along with Canada, Mexico, and Central America. The United States has fifty states.

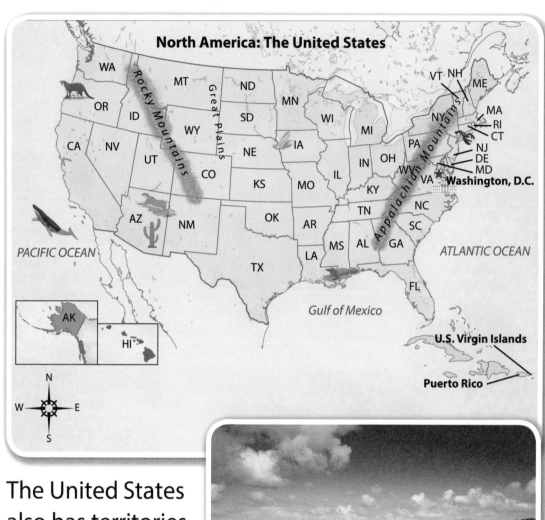

North America: The United States

WA · MT · ND · MN · VT · NH · ME

Rocky Mountains

Great Plains

OR · ID · SD · WI · NY · MA · RI · CT

CA · NV · WY · NE · IA · MI · PA · NJ · DE · MD

UT · CO · KS · MO · IL · IN · OH · WV · VA · Washington, D.C.

Appalachian Mountains

AZ · NM · OK · AR · TN · KY · NC · SC

MS · AL · GA

LA · TX

FL

PACIFIC OCEAN

ATLANTIC OCEAN

Gulf of Mexico

AK · HI

N · W · E · S

U.S. Virgin Islands

Puerto Rico

The United States also has territories, such as Puerto Rico and the U.S. Virgin Islands in a region known as the Caribbean. There are beautiful beaches in the U.S. Virgin Islands.

The United States is a country with its own government and laws. The government for the United States is in the capital city, Washington, D.C. Members of the government meet in

the Capitol Building. The president lives in the White House, which is also in Washington, D.C.

If you were to travel across the United States, you would see many different kinds of landscapes. For example, most New England states have beautiful coastlines. Some New England states have mountains and lakes. The United States has many large cities, such as New York City, where millions of people live.

If you traveled to the southern part of the United States, you would find that it is hotter there than in the North. The South has beautiful beaches. People like to vacation in Florida, a state that is a long peninsula. The Midwest has cornfields and dairy farms.

If you visited the Great Plains, you would see that there are miles and miles of flat land where wheat is grown. The Rocky Mountain region has—you guessed it—tall mountains that stretch across a large part of North America. The Southwest has canyons and deserts, and the West Coast has an awesome coastline.

To get to Alaska you would have to drive or fly across Canada. In terms of land, Alaska is the largest U.S. state. The weather there is really quite cold. The state of Hawaii is made up of a number of tropical islands two thousand miles away from California, in the Pacific Ocean. How might you get to Hawaii?

North America: Canada, Mexico, and Central America

Canada is on the northern border of the United States. It is the second largest country in the world. However, fewer people live in Canada than in the United States because the northern part of the country is often icy and cold. There are two main languages in Canada—English and French. The capital of Canada is Ottawa.

Native Canadians, named the Inuit, live in the far north of Canada, in the Canadian Arctic. They have lived there for a very long time and know how to hunt, fish, and survive in the ice and snow. Polar bears live there too!

Mexico is on the southern border of the United States. It is a land of high mountains, dry deserts, leafy rainforests, and a large central plateau. Mexico has volcanoes too. Most people live on the central plateau because the land there is good for farming. Mexican farmers grow crops such as corn, sugarcane, wheat, avocados, tropical fruits, and coffee.

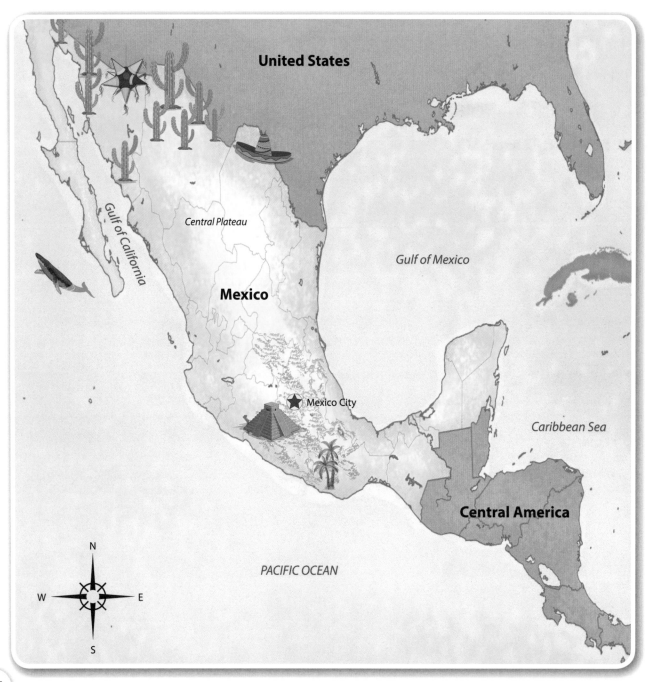

United States

Central Plateau

Gulf of California

Gulf of Mexico

Mexico

Mexico City

Caribbean Sea

Central America

PACIFIC OCEAN

N
W E
S

Mexico has thirty-one states. Its capital is Mexico City, one of the largest cities in the world. Many people in Mexico speak Spanish, though some people also speak the languages of their Aztec and Maya ancestors. Mexican people enjoy celebrating their culture, which is rich in food, music, dance, and art.

To the south of Mexico is Central America. This long, narrow area of land connects North America and South America. There are seven small countries in Central America.

CENTRAL AMERICA

Belize

Guatemala

Honduras

Lake Atitlán

El Salvador

Nicaragua

Caribbean Sea

PACIFIC OCEAN

Costa Rica

N
W   E
S

Panama

Nicaragua is the largest country in Central America, and El Salvador is the smallest.

Central America has mountains and volcanoes. It has beautiful beaches and green rainforests. Farmers in Central America grow coffee, bananas, and pineapples.

In the waters of the Caribbean Sea, near Florida in the United States and northern South America, there are a number of islands called the West Indies. One of these islands, Puerto Rico, is part of the United States. The capital of Puerto Rico is San Juan.

South America

There are twelve countries on the continent of South America. The largest country in South America is Brazil, and the smallest country is Suriname.

The Amazon Rainforest in South America is the largest rainforest in the world. This rainforest is almost as big as the whole of the United States.

Thousands of people and many different kinds of animals and plants live in the Amazon Rainforest. There are electric eels, poisonous arrow frogs, and slithering snakes. There are also giant lily pads that can hold the weight of an adult person. The mighty Amazon River flows through the center of the Amazon Rainforest. It is the second longest river in the world.

The Kayapo are a group of people who have lived in the Amazon Rainforest of Brazil for thousands of years. They are a warrior tribe. The Kayapo are expert hunters and fishermen. They also gather food, such as nuts and berries, from the rainforest.

The Andes Mountains make up the longest mountain range in the world. This mountain range is on the western coast of South America and is in seven of the South American countries. The highest volcano in the world, Ojos del Salado, is in the Andes.

There are ancient and modern cities in the Andes Mountains. High up on top of a mountain in southern Peru, ruins remain of an ancient city that was built by the Inca, who lived there long ago. This city is called Machu Picchu. La Paz in Bolivia is a busy, modern city in the Andes.

Europe

Europe is the second smallest continent in size. There are forty-four countries in Europe. The largest country is Russia, and the smallest is Vatican City. But as you will discover, Russia is not only in Europe—it is also in Asia.

Each European country has its own customs, government, laws, and languages. And each European country has its own landscape. For example, the country of Ireland is on an island, while the country of Austria is on the continent of Europe and is mostly covered in mountains.

Moscow, the capital of Russia, is the largest city in Europe. Russia also has the Volga River, which is the longest river in Europe, and Mount Elbrus, which is the highest mountain. And you guessed it! Lake Ladoga, the largest lake in Europe, is in Russia too!

In addition to Moscow, there are many other beautiful cities in Europe. Some of these cities are known for their famous landmarks. Paris, the capital of France, has the Eiffel Tower. The clock tower, Big Ben, is in London, the capital of the United Kingdom. The ancient Greek Acropolis is in the Greek capital of Athens. And the ancient Roman Colosseum is in the Italian capital of Rome.

Africa and Asia

Africa is the second largest continent in the world, and it has the second highest number of people. There are fifty-four countries in Africa, with more than fifteen hundred spoken languages. Like Europe, each African country has its own government and laws. Algeria is the largest country, and the Seychelles, a country made up of islands, is the smallest.

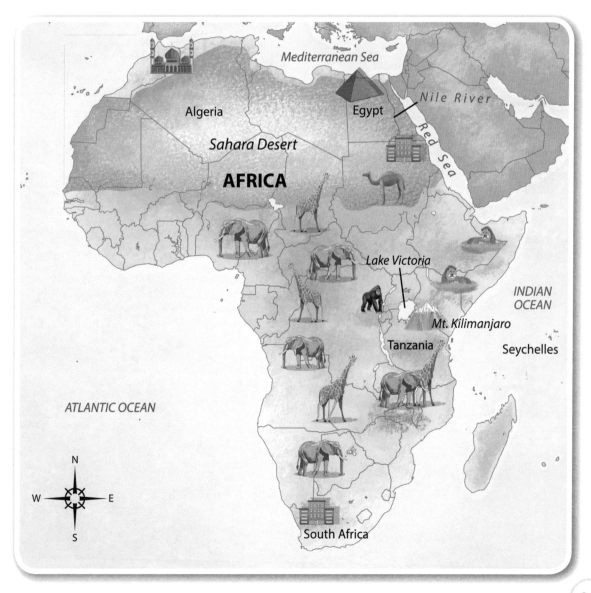

Africa has busy, modern cities with thousands of people rushing here and there. The modern city of Luxor, on the bank of Egypt's Nile River, was built on the site of an ancient Egyptian city. Today, you see the old and the new side by side. Cape Town, in South Africa, is the southernmost city on the African continent.

The longest river in the world, the Nile River, is in Africa, and the largest hot desert, the Sahara, is there too. Africa also has Lake Victoria, the second largest lake in the world. Africa's highest mountain is Mount Kilimanjaro. The giraffe, the tallest land animal in the world, lives in Africa.

Asia is the largest continent in the world. There are forty-eight countries in Asia. It is the most populated continent, and more than two thousand languages are spoken there.

Russia is not only the largest country in Europe, but it is also the largest country in Asia. In fact, Russia is the largest country in the world. China has more people than any other country though. The Maldives, a group of islands, is the smallest Asian country.

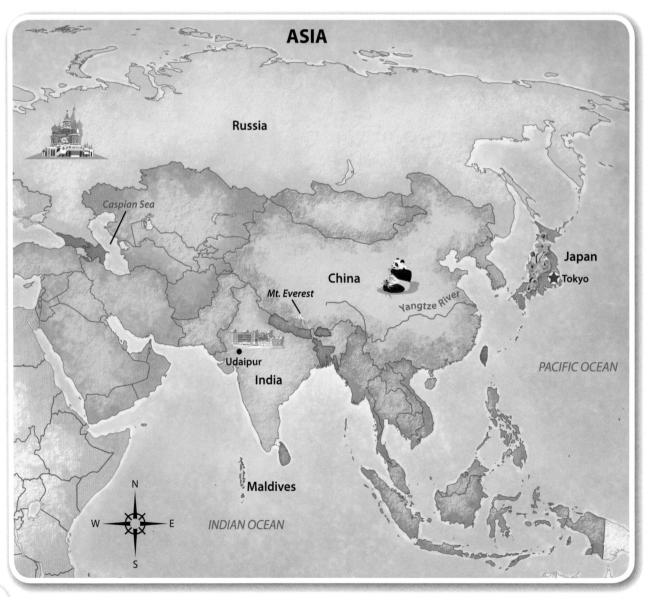

The highest mountain in the world, Mount Everest, is in Asia. Mount Everest is five and a half miles high. The largest lake in the world is a body of water called the Caspian Sea. Like Russia, this lake is in both Europe and Asia. The longest river in Asia is the Chinese Yangtze River. The giant panda lives in the bamboo forests of China.

Tokyo is the capital city of Japan. More than thirty-eight million people live in the city. In springtime in Japan, people celebrate the cherry blossoms that flower at this time.

Udaipur in India is known as the City of Lakes. This beautiful, walled Indian city is a popular place for people from all over the world to visit.

CHAPTER 7

Australia and Antarctica

The country of Australia is an island *and* a continent. It is the smallest of all the continents. Australia is the sixth largest country in the world. The capital of Australia is Canberra. A large part of Australia is hot, dry desert called the Outback. Because of this, Australia does not have a large population, and most people live near the coast.

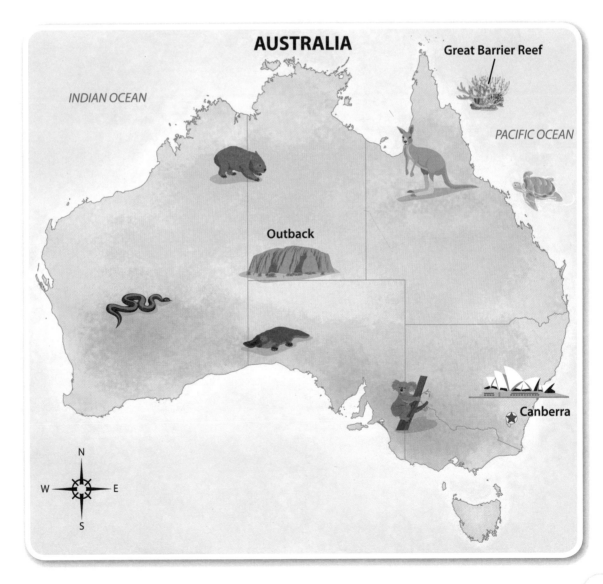

Australia is surrounded by the Indian Ocean and the Pacific Ocean. The Great Barrier Reef is just off the coast of Australia. It is the largest coral reef in the world. This means it is the largest living thing on Earth. The Great Barrier Reef can be seen from space.

More than 80 percent of the plants and wildlife found in Australia can only be found there. This includes many poisonous snakes, as well as kangaroos and koala bears. And there is even an Australian fish called the lungfish that lived during the time of dinosaurs!

Australia's Aboriginal people have lived in Australia for thousands of years. Aboriginal people know how to survive in the hot, dry Outback. They can find food and water in the most unlikely places. Aboriginal people have a tradition of telling stories. They pass down their history and their knowledge of the land in this way.

Antarctica is the southernmost continent and is the fifth largest. It is the coldest, windiest, and driest continent. There are mountains in Antarctica, and there's even a volcano under the ice. Scientists and some tourists go to Antarctica to learn about this frozen land.

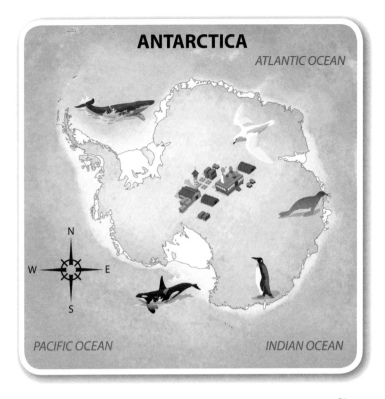

Penguins are birds that live in Antarctica. Penguins cannot fly, but they are really good swimmers. Seals live in Antarctica too.

Fun Facts

 Shanghai in China has a professional baseball team called the Golden Eagles.

 People in Japan like vending machines so much that you can buy everything from candy to clothes in these machines.

 There are three times as many sheep in Australia as people.

 The coldest temperature ever officially recorded was recorded in Antarctica. It was minus 128.6 F°.

 Europe is the only continent without a desert.

 The world's largest wildlife migration occurs in Africa. Almost two million animals travel across the Serengeti, a huge grassland area in eastern Africa.

 The world's longest annual dogsled race, the Iditarod, occurs every year in Alaska. It commemorates the race to deliver medicine to the Alaskan town of Nome.

 The Great Barrier Reef is the size of seventy million football fields.

 Planet Earth moves around the sun at 67,000 miles per hour and is about 93 million miles away from the sun.

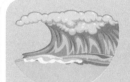 Oceans cover 70 percent of planet Earth.

 Every day, planet Earth is sprinkled with lots of dust from space.

 There was once a supercontinent called Pangaea at a time when all the land was joined together.

CKHG™

Core Knowledge HISTORY AND GEOGRAPHY™

Editorial Directors

Linda Bevilacqua and Rosie McCormick

Subject Matter Expert

Charles F. Gritzner, PhD

Distinguished Professor Emeritus of Geography, South Dakota State University

Illustration and Photo Credits